CO

C000070253

Ina Scheurwater

FORTE PUBLISHERS

Contents

ISBN 90 5877 373 6

This is a publication from
Forte Publishers BV
P.O. Box 1394
3500 BJ Utrecht
The Netherlands

For more information about the
creative books available from
Forte Publishers:
www.hobby-party.com

Publisher: Els Neele
Editor: Gina Kors-Lambers
Photography and digital image
editing: Piet Pulles Fotografie,
Waalwijk, the Netherlands
Cover and inner design
BADE creatieve communicatie, Baarn,
the Netherlands
Translation: TextCase, Groningen,
the Netherlands

Preface

It has been great fun making this second book about 'Line embossing'.

Lots of people have asked me when it would be published. Well, here it is.

I have done my best to make plenty of variations, leaving enough room

for your own creativity. I wish you all lots of fun with this publication.

Ina Scheurwater

Thanks

I owe many thanks to Mr G. Nederlof of Oegstgeest who processed my text on a computer.

Techniques

General method for embossing

Secure the embossing stencil to the light box using adhesive tape. Next, place the card on the stencil with the good side facing the stencil and secure it in place using some adhesive tape. Turn the light on. First, gently push the embossing pen between the open lines and then push a little harder. Use the thin point for the really narrow lines. If the card needs to be stippled, do this before removing the card from the stencil. Cut individual pieces out leaving a 2 mm border. Do this carefully and always rotate the paper whilst keeping the scissors still. Round off all the points to finish it off nicely.

Tip:
It is easier to emboss using a smooth pen. You can use Pergasoft, a candle or dry toilet soap to make the pen smooth.

Stippling with stamp-pad ink

Apply a small amount of ink to a foam brush or a small piece of sponge and rub this up and down the embossed lines. Use a different brush or sponge for each colour. Tear thin paper into

pieces and use them to cover the parts which must not be touched. When you are finished, clean the stencil with a tissue.

Tip:
To apply the glue in small beads, use a cocktail stick to remove a small bead from the glue gun and stick this behind small petals etc.

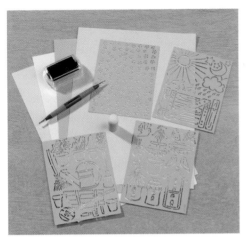

1. Materials required for Line embossing.

2. Use Pergasoft, a candle or dry toilet soap to emboss more smoothly.

3. When cutting stippled sections, always leave a 2 mm border.

4. Cut out loose sections and stick them on the card using beads of glue.

Materials

- ☐ A4 220-gram card
- ☐ Vellum (patterned)
- ☐ Line embossing stencils
  LE 2407 to LE 2412
- ☐ Line embossing tool
- ☐ Light box
- ☐ Colorbox paintbox
  stamp-pad ink
- ☐ Foam brushes
- ☐ Pergasoft or a candle

- ☐ Cutting mat
- ☐ Knife
- ☐ Ruler
- ☐ Scissors
- ☐ Photo adhesive
- ☐ Adhesive tape
  (removable tape)
- ☐ Glue (silicon or 3D)
- ☐ Ribbons and string

The other materials are stated
with the relevant chapters.
The sizes of the double cards are
10 x 15 cm and 13 x 13 cm, unless
specified otherwise.

Orange cards

What you need
- ☐ Line embossing stencil LE 2408
- ☐ Artoz card white 211
- ☐ Artoz card black 219
- ☐ Artoz card bright red 549
- ☐ Aslan double-sided adhesive film
- ☐ Figure punch butterfly
- ☐ Figure punch corner rounder C

Card 1

Make a bright red card of 7 x 7.5 cm. Punch out the corners. Stick this card in the left top corner on a double portrait card. Cut and punch a similar card of black card. Stick this in the bottom centre. Colour a scrap piece of white paper orange by putting some orange stamp-pad ink on a foam brush. First remove any excess ink by wiping the brush on a tissue or napkin. Now lightly stroke the paper until you have the colour that you want. It must look flamed. Now emboss three flowers on this paper and cut them out leaving a small border. Do the same with a white card of 7 x 7.5 cm and stamp-pad ink and punch out the corners. Emboss the entire flower pattern on it. Perforate three red hearts and stick them on the flowers. Slightly bend the petals of the flowers

that you have cut out. Place a bead of glue behind every petal and a dab of glue behind the heart of the flower. Arrange them on the orange card (only push down the heart). Stick the orange card on the card, using beads of glue. Punch out two butterflies, glue them using Aslan and bend their wings up.

Card 2

Extra materials
☐ *Bradletz orange*

Make a bright red card of 10.5 x 15 cm, fold it double and stick it on the double white card. Make a white card of 5 x 13.5 cm and make it flaming orange as described for card 1. Emboss the flower pattern on this card three times. Stick this on a slightly larger black card and arrange this on the card as shown in the photograph. Now make a scrap piece of card flaming orange, emboss three flowers and cut them out leaving a small border. Bend the petals up a bit, and place a bead of glue behind each petal and a dab of glue behind the heart of the flower. Push the heart of the flower onto the card. Emboss a text on an orange scrap piece of 1.6 x 4.3 cm. Stipple the text in slightly darker orange with a little black border at the bottom. Run the sides along the stamp pad. This way you will create a

nice finish. Hang the card using a bradlet. Apply a bead of glue in the right bottom corner at the back of the card.

Card 3

Extra materials
☐ *Bradletz orange*

Make a bright red card of 9.5 x 9.5 cm. Punch out the corners, and stick this in the left top corner, at 1 cm from the edge, on a double square card. Make a white card of 9 x 9 cm and make it flaming orange as described for card 1. Cut this into four squares of 4.5 x 4.5 cm. Run the outsides along the stamp pad (see card 2). Punch out the corners. Emboss the flower pattern on two cards and emboss two loose flowers on a scrap piece. Cut out the individual flowers leaving a small border. Stick the squares on some black card of 9.7 x 9.7 cm. Stick this all in the right bottom corner, at 1 cm from the edge. Bend the petals up a bit, and put a bead of glue behind each petal and a dab of glue behind the heart of the flower. Only push the heart of the flower onto the card. Place two bradletz or punch out two red hearts.

1.

2.

3.

Flowers with background

What you need
- [ ] Line embossing stencil LE 2408
- [ ] Artoz card cornflower 425
- [ ] Papicolor card lilac 37
- [ ] Transparent embossing powder
- [ ] Figure punch butterfly
- [ ] Punch Paper Weaving (Avec)

Card 1

Tear a large strip from a single blue card. Hold your left thumb firmly in the place where you start tearing. Slowly tear away the section above your thumb with your right hand, so that a thin layer of paper also comes loose. Stick this on a landscape card. Tear off a narrower lilac-coloured slanting strip in the same manner. Emboss the flower stalks with leaves at various heights on this section, so that the flowers will extend beyond the torn edge. Emboss and stipple five flowers. Sprinkle transparent embossing powder over the embossed parts and hold them over a toaster until the powder has melted and has become shiny. Cut out the flowers. Apply a bead of glue behind every petal. Push the heart of the flower onto the card. Punch out coloured butterflies to finish the card.

Card 2

Cut a strip of lilac card of 8 x 15 cm. Punch holes in the sides or make 1 cm wide incisions. Thread an 0.8 cm wide strip of paper through the holes or incisions. Emboss some leaves at random places between the holes (using the same stencil). Stick this on a portrait card. Emboss and stipple three flowers completely and three partially (always first stipple before removing the stencil). Sprinkle transparent embossing powder over the embossed parts and hold them over a toaster until the powder has melted and has become shiny. Cut everything out. First secure the bottom flower using glue and then stick the smaller section on top of it using a bead of glue for every petal.

Card 3

Make a blue card of 11 x 11 cm. Punch out the corners and emboss lines in between. Stick this on a double lilac-coloured card of 12 cm. Make four lilac-coloured cards of 4 x 4 cm and punch out the corners. Emboss some leaves (using the same stencil) in random places on two squares. Emboss and stipple the flower on the other two squares and emboss and stipple two further flowers on a scrap piece. Stipple them before removing the stencil. Treat the card with embossing powder (see card 1). Cut out the loose flowers. Bend the petals up, put some glue under them and stick them both on the embossed flowers. Apply the squares, raised a bit, as shown in the photograph.

Blue and pink flower cards

What you need
- ☐ *Line embossing stencils LE 2411 and LE 2408*
- ☐ *Artoz card pink 481*
- ☐ *Artoz card royal blue 427*

them round. Apply everything in 3D, as shown in the photograph. Stick it all on a double blue card of 12.5 x 12.5 cm. Make a card with text and stick this on the card.

Card 1

Make a pink card of 7 x 12.5 cm. Emboss a line on both sides at 0.5 cm from the edge. Emboss

and stipple the bouquet of roses on the card. There must be 5 cm left above the bouquet. Emboss and stipple another half bouquet, a rose, the basket without the handle and a watering can. Cut out the loose parts. Bend the basket and the watering can slightly to make

Card 2

Extra materials
- ☐ *Line embossing stencil LE 2407*
- ☐ *Cassette Craft punch holder with alphabet*

Make a pink card of 8.5 x 8.5 cm. Emboss diagonal lines up to halfway the card (see card 3). Punch out the 'Best wishes' text twice. Emboss and stipple the entire central flower on a scrap piece, followed by only the flower and the two smaller flowers (first stipple before removing the stencil). Cut everything out. Bend up all petals, put a bead of glue behind them and stick them on the card as shown in the photograph. Secure the heart of the flower with a dab of glue. Stick this all on a somewhat larger blue card. Emboss a 3 cm wide border of leaves and flowers along the fold and the top on the front of a double pink card (stencil LE 2407). Stick the small card in the right bottom corner on the double card, using small beads of glue.

Card 3

Make a pink card of 8 x 8 cm. Emboss eight diagonal lines from the corners, so that they meet in the centre. If you have no stencil for embossing straight lines, you can make one by cutting a strip of 2 mm out of a coloured plastic sleeve. Use a fineliner pen to draw a line at 0.5 cm above the strip. This is the half centimetre that is always between the lines. Make a white card of 4.5 x 5.5 cm and emboss the vase with tulips on it. Emboss the vase and the two budding flowers on a scrap piece. Cut

them out, bend them a little and secure them using a bead of glue. Make a card of 1.3 x 3.5 cm and cut off the corners diagonally. Emboss and stipple a text on it. Secure this with photo adhesive and put a bead of glue under the end. Stick this on a blue card of 5.9 x 5.9 cm. Raise it with glue and stick it on the pink card. Stick it all on a blue card of 13 x 13 cm.

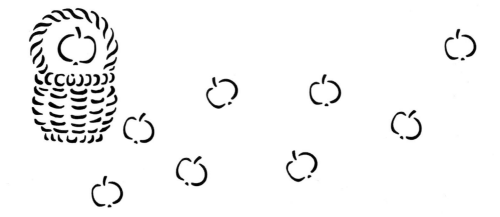

Silhouette cards

What you need
- ☐ Line embossing stencil LE 2412
- ☐ Artoz card dark blue 417
- ☐ Artoz card pastel green 331

Card 1

Make a dark blue card of 8.5 x 8.5 cm. Stick this on a double pastel green card. Make a pastel green card of 8 x 4 cm. Emboss the butterfly to exactly halfway the card. Very carefully cut out the butterfly leaving a little border. Stick the section that you have cut out on the right and the butterfly on the left. Raise the butterfly using glue.

Card 2

Make a pastel green strip of 5 x 15 cm. Emboss the two butterflies to exactly halfway the card. Very carefully cut them out leaving a little border. Stick the section that you have cut out on the left of the card (1.4 cm from the fold). Stick the two butterflies against this, using a bead of glue. Stick the body on the card. Cut another narrow strip of blue and stick this on the left on the green card.

Card 3

Extra materials
- ☐ Line embossing stencil LE 2408

Make a pastel green card of 5.3 x 15 cm. Emboss three flowers to exactly halfway the card. Very carefully cut them out leaving a little border. Emboss three half flowers along the folding edge. Stick this card on a double blue card. Stick the flowers that you have cut out carefully against it. Apply a bead of glue behind every petal.

Garden cards

What you need
- ☐ *Line embossing stencil LE 2411*
- ☐ *Artoz card pink 481*
- ☐ *Artoz card wine red 519*
- ☐ *Vellum flower fairies 1*
- ☐ *Figure punch butterfly*
- ☐ *Aslan double-sided adhesive film*
- ☐ *Ribbon*

Card 1

Cut off half the front of a double pink card. Emboss the entire flowerpot in the right bottom corner and emboss three flowers and two flowerpots on a scrap piece. Cut out all individual pieces leaving a small border. Stick an 0.4 cm wide red border in the centre, at the bottom. Bend the pots a little and apply the loose parts in 3D. Cut vellum of 10.5 x 15 cm and fold it double. Stick a strip of 0.5 cm Aslan along the fold on the rear. Slide the card between the vellum that you have folded double, pull the protective layer from the Aslan and rub the vellum onto it. Stick some Aslan on the front, at the same level as the watering can. Emboss the watering can, cut it out leaving a small border, bend it slightly and stick it on the card using a considerably sized bead of glue.

Finish the card by sticking a little red bow tie and two vellum butterflies on it.

Card 2

Extra materials
☐ Line embossing stencil LE 2407

Cut off 5.5 cm of the front of a double pink card.
Stick an 0.8 cm wide red border along the cut
edge. Emboss petals on the rest of the front.
Make a backing card of 13 x 13 cm. Stick a strip
of vellum of 6.5 cm wide on the right of this
backing card by sticking small bits of Aslan
under the dark flower hearts. Stick the backing
card against the half front. Emboss a watering
can, a broom and a bucket. Cut them out
leaving a small border. Slightly bend all the
parts. Stick everything in 3D on the card, using
beads of glue. A bow tie and butterflies finish
this off nicely.

Card 3

Extra materials
☐ Eyelets red

Make a pink card of 10.5 x 17 cm and make a
10.5 x 15 cm vellum card. Fold both cards
double and put them around the fold of the
double landscape card. Apply two eyelets at
1 cm from the fold, leaving a 3 cm space in
between. Tie a ribbon through these eyelets.
Emboss a wheelbarrow, two pots with extra top
rims, a spade, a lever and three plants (without
pots). Cut everything out leaving a small border.
Bend all the parts that need to be bent. First
stick the wheelbarrow on the card with three
plants in it, using glue. Stick the lever on the
card with photo adhesive. Stick the two pots in
the bottom right corner using glue; use photo
adhesive for the double rim. Now put the spade
in front of the wheelbarrow, behind the wheel.
Decorate the card with three butterflies.

1.

2.

3.

Pink spring cards

What you need
- ☐ *Line embossing stencil LE 2412*
- ☐ *Artoz card pink 481*
- ☐ *Artoz card wine red 519*
- ☐ *Eyelets red*

Card 1

Make a pink strip of 4.5 x 12.5 cm and two strips of 1.5 x 12.5 cm. Emboss a line on all six long sides at 0.5 cm from the edge. Emboss three butterflies on the wide strip and three butterflies without antennae on a scrap piece of card. Cut them out. Bend the wings. Place a bead of glue behind them; put only a dab of glue on the body. Stick the strips on a double red card, 0.5 cm apart. Punch two eyelets with shapes in the right-hand bottom corner.

Card 2

Emboss the entire flower on a pink card of 8.5 x 8.5 cm and emboss the petals and the flower on a scrap piece. Stipple the heart of the flower using red stamp-pad ink (before removing the stencil). Cut out the flower and the petals. Bend up the petals and put a bead of glue behind every petal. Slightly bend the petals and stick them on the card using glue. Punch eyelets with shapes in the four corners. Stick the pink card diagonally on a red card of 9.5 x 9.5 cm and stick them together on a double pink card.

Card 3

Emboss a line all round the front of the double pink card at 0.7 cm from the edge.
Stick a red strip of 5 x 10.5 cm in the frame that you have now created. Emboss the bellflower on a pink card of 7 x 8.5 cm and emboss four bells on a scrap piece.
Cut them out, bend them a little and apply them using a bead of glue. Punch red eyelets in the corners. Put some beads of glue on this small card and stick it on the double card.

Marble butterfly cards

What you need
- [ ] *Line embossing stencil LE 2412*
- [ ] *Artoz card royal blue 427*
- [ ] *Artoz card pastel blue 413*
- [ ] *Satin cord*

Card 1

Make a royal blue card of 7 x 12.5 cm. Stick this on a double pastel blue card of 12.5 x 12.5 cm. Make a white card of 6.5 x 6.5 cm and punch out the corners. Treat this card and a scrap piece with blue stamp-pad ink as described for the 'Orange' cards. Emboss one butterfly on the card and one on a scrap piece. Cut out the butterfly leaving a small border. Bend the wings up slightly. Put two beads of glue behind every wing; put only a dab of glue on the body. Push the body onto the small card. Stick the small card in the right bottom corner on the double card, at 1.5 cm from the edge, using well-sized beads of glue. Punch out two holes, thread a blue cord through them. Tie knots in the ends of the cord and unravel them.

Card 2

Make a pastel blue card of 5 x 12.5 cm and stick it on a double royal blue card of 12.5 x 12.5 cm (fold at the top). Make two white cards of 4.5 x 4.5 cm. Treat these cards and a scrap piece with some blue stamp-pad ink (see card 1). Emboss a flying butterfly on both cards and emboss two more butterflies without antennae on a scrap piece (leave out the upper line of the rearmost wing). Note: the butterflies are facing each other, so rotate the stencil for the second butterfly. Cut them out leaving a small border. Bend the wings up slightly, place two well-sized beads of glue behind them and apply a dab of

glue on the bodies. Push the bodies onto the cards. Stick the cards on a somewhat larger blue card. Punch a hole in the centre of the card, at 1 cm from the fold and punch a hole in both small cards. Fold one blue cord double and thread it through the card from the rear to the front. Thread both cords through this loop. Hang the cards from the ends, determine their heights and tie a knot. Cut the cord and unravel the ends. Stick the small cards on a double card, using some glue.

Card 3

Make a royal blue card of 7.3 x 12.5 cm. Stick this on a double pastel blue card of 12.5 x 12.5 cm, at 0.7 cm from the fold. Cut off a strip

on the right, leaving a 0.7 cm border. Stick a royal blue strip of 4.5 cm on the lower card, on the right. Make a white card of 6.8 x 12.5 cm and a square of 6 x 6 cm. Decorate these cards and a scrap piece with some blue stamp-pad ink (see card 1). Emboss one butterfly on the square card and one on a scrap piece (without antennae). Cut them out leaving a small border. Bend the wings up, place two beads of glue behind them and apply a smear of glue behind the body. Push the body onto the card. Stick the card of 6.8 x 12.5 cm on the left on the blue card. Stick the square card on a somewhat larger blue card. Punch two holes on the left and the right in the small card. Tie a cord through them and unravel the ends of the cord. Stick the small card on the left of the card, using glue.

Bird cards

Card 1

Tear a hill from grey card, as described for 'Flowers with a background', card 1. Stick this on a double blue card. Apply a silver sticker border at 2.5 cm from the top fold. Emboss five birds and cut them out leaving a little border. Cut incisions into the wings. Bend the wings up a little and bend the birds to make them round. Place all five of them on the line, using a bead of glue. Stick two hearts between the two birds on the left. Emboss and stipple a bird table, three flowers, three leaves and a drinking bowl with a bird. Cut out all individual pieces leaving a small border. Bend the flowers up and bend the other parts to make them round. Stick some silver card behind the drinking bowl. Punch or perforate a hole in the bird table. Secure everything using glue (only secure the hearts of the flowers). Stick the thatched roof just over the cutting line.

Card 2

Make two hills (see card 1). Stick the first one on a double square blue card. Bend the second one slightly round. Put a well-sized bead of glue on the centre and a dab of glue on both sides. Stick this on the first one. Emboss and stipple three birds, the feeding table (the front of the pot extra), three flowers and a flying bird. Cut out all individual pieces leaving a small border. Cut incisions into the wings. Stick everything on

the card, using beads of glue. Check card 1 again if necessary. Stick hearts between the two lower birds.

Card 3

Tear some paper to make a hill that runs from high to low (see card 1). Stick it on a double blue card. Emboss and stipple two bird tables, two sitting birds, one flying bird, three flowers and a water bowl. Cut out all individual pieces leaving a small border. Punch or perforate a hole in both bird tables. Finish the parts as described for card 1.

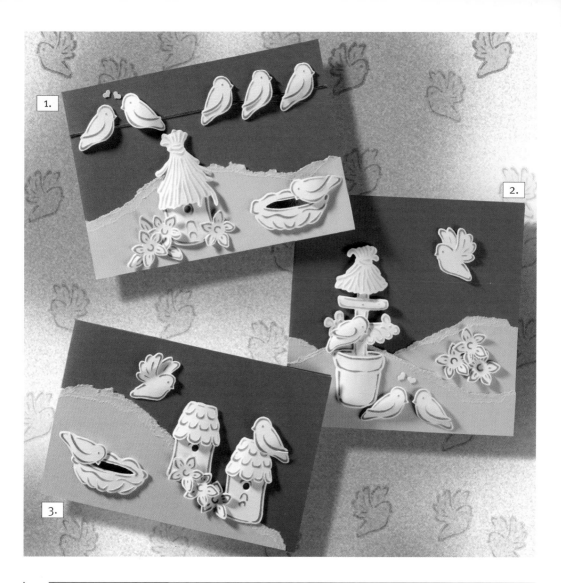

1.

2.

3.

Collage cards with flowers

Card 1

What you need
- ☐ *Line embossing stencil LE 2411*
- ☐ *Artoz card fawn 241*
- ☐ *Artoz card wine red 519*
- ☐ *Eyelets red*
- ☐ *Corner ornament punch heart*
- ☐ *Figure punch corner rounder C*
- ☐ *String*

Make a red card of 8.5 x 11.5 cm. Punch out two corners and stick it on a double yellow card Now make a yellow card of 8.5 x 6.3 cm. Emboss a border at 0.5 cm from the edge. Emboss and stipple the entire flowerpot on this card and emboss three loose tulips on a scrap piece. Cut them out and stick them on the card using a bead of glue. Stick the card as shown in the photograph as soon as the glue

has dried. Fold the card open and punch two eyelets in the left of the small card, through three layers. Thread a string through them.

Card 2

What you need
- ☐ *Line embossing stencil LE 2411*
- ☐ *Artoz card fir green 339*
- ☐ *Artoz card royal blue 427*
- ☐ *Figure punch corner rounder C*
- ☐ *Aslan double-sided adhesive film*

Make a green square of 9 x 9 cm. Punch out the corners and stick it on a double blue card. Emboss and stipple an entire flowerpot on a 5 x 5.2 cm card and emboss and stipple three loose flowers on a scrap piece. Cut out the flowers. Secure the flowers, using little beads of glue. Stick a suitable bow tie on the flowerpot, using double-sided Aslan. Stick this all on a slightly larger blue card as soon as the glue has dried. Stick this card on the green square, using some beads of glue.

Card 3

What you need
- ☐ *Line embossing stencil LE 2411*
- ☐ *Artoz card dark blue 417*
- ☐ *Artoz card pearl-grey 215*
- ☐ *Figure punch corner rounder C*
- ☐ *Ribbon*

Cut a grey strip of 17 x 8.5 cm and fold it double. Score a line at 3 cm from the fold (only the front). Punch out the corners. Make a blue and a grey card of 4.5 x 5.5 cm. Punch out these corners too. Emboss and stipple the pot of tulips on the grey card and emboss and stipple a loose flowerpot. Bend the pot slightly, put some glue behind it and stick it on the card. Apply the cards, as shown in the photograph. Slightly raise the grey card using glue. Punch out two holes between the fold and the scoring line, 4 cm apart. Thread a matching ribbon through this and tie it in a bow tie. Stick this all on a double blue card.

Thanks to the Kars company for providing the materials.

Shopkeepers can order the materials from Kars & Co B.V., Ochten, the Netherlands